Welcome

Messages

GUEST NAME ______________________ DATE(S) STAYED ______________________

TRAVELING FROM ______________________

OUR FAV MEMORY OR RECOMMENDED ACTIVITY

MY MESSAGE

MAY WE SHARE YOUR MESSAGE? ☐ YES ☐ NO

Messages

GUEST NAME

DATE(S) STAYED

TRAVELING FROM

OUR FAV MEMORY OR RECOMMENDED ACTIVITY

MY MESSAGE

MAY WE SHARE YOUR MESSAGE? ☐ YES ☐ NO

Messages

GUEST NAME ______________________ DATE(S) STAYED ______________________

TRAVELING FROM ______________________

OUR FAV MEMORY OR RECOMMENDED ACTIVITY

MY MESSAGE

MAY WE SHARE YOUR MESSAGE? ☐ YES ☐ NO

Messages

GUEST NAME ______________________ DATE(S) STAYED ______________________

TRAVELING FROM ______________________

OUR FAV MEMORY OR RECOMMENDED ACTIVITY

MY MESSAGE

MAY WE SHARE YOUR MESSAGE? ☐ YES ☐ NO

Messages

GUEST NAME ____________ DATE(S) STAYED ____________

TRAVELING FROM ____________

OUR FAV MEMORY OR RECOMMENDED ACTIVITY

MY MESSAGE

MAY WE SHARE YOUR MESSAGE? ☐ YES ☐ NO

Messages

GUEST NAME ______________ DATE(S) STAYED ______________

TRAVELING FROM ______________

OUR FAV MEMORY OR RECOMMENDED ACTIVITY

MY MESSAGE

MAY WE SHARE YOUR MESSAGE? ☐ YES ☐ NO

Messages

GUEST NAME ______________________ DATE(S) STAYED ______________________

TRAVELING FROM ______________________

OUR FAV MEMORY OR RECOMMENDED ACTIVITY

MY MESSAGE

MAY WE SHARE YOUR MESSAGE? ☐ YES ☐ NO

Messages

GUEST NAME

DATE(S) STAYED

TRAVELING FROM

OUR FAV MEMORY OR RECOMMENDED ACTIVITY

MY MESSAGE

MAY WE SHARE YOUR MESSAGE? ☐ YES ☐ NO

Messages

GUEST NAME DATE(S) STAYED

TRAVELING FROM

OUR FAV MEMORY OR RECOMMENDED ACTIVITY

MY MESSAGE

MAY WE SHARE YOUR MESSAGE? YES NO

Messages

GUEST NAME ______________________ DATE(S) STAYED ______________________

TRAVELING FROM ______________________

OUR FAV MEMORY OR RECOMMENDED ACTIVITY

MY MESSAGE

MAY WE SHARE YOUR MESSAGE? ☐ YES ☐ NO

Messages

GUEST NAME

DATE(S) STAYED

TRAVELING FROM

OUR FAV MEMORY OR RECOMMENDED ACTIVITY

MY MESSAGE

MAY WE SHARE YOUR MESSAGE? ☐ YES ☐ NO

Messages

GUEST NAME

DATE(S) STAYED

TRAVELING FROM

OUR FAV MEMORY OR RECOMMENDED ACTIVITY

MY MESSAGE

MAY WE SHARE YOUR MESSAGE? ☐ YES ☐ NO

Messages

GUEST NAME DATE(S) STAYED

TRAVELING FROM

OUR FAV MEMORY OR RECOMMENDED ACTIVITY

MY MESSAGE

MAY WE SHARE YOUR MESSAGE? ☐ YES ☐ NO

Messages

GUEST NAME

DATE(S) STAYED

TRAVELING FROM

OUR FAV MEMORY OR RECOMMENDED ACTIVITY

MY MESSAGE

MAY WE SHARE YOUR MESSAGE? ☐ YES ☐ NO

Messages

GUEST NAME ____________ DATE(S) STAYED ____________

TRAVELING FROM ____________

OUR FAV MEMORY OR RECOMMENDED ACTIVITY

MY MESSAGE

MAY WE SHARE YOUR MESSAGE? ☐ YES ☐ NO

Messages

GUEST NAME

DATE(S) STAYED

TRAVELING FROM

OUR FAV MEMORY OR RECOMMENDED ACTIVITY

MY MESSAGE

MAY WE SHARE YOUR MESSAGE? ☐ YES ☐ NO

Messages

GUEST NAME ______________________ DATE(S) STAYED ______________________

TRAVELING FROM ______________________

OUR FAV MEMORY OR RECOMMENDED ACTIVITY

MY MESSAGE

MAY WE SHARE YOUR MESSAGE? ☐ YES ☐ NO

Messages

GUEST NAME ____________ DATE(S) STAYED ____________

TRAVELING FROM ____________

OUR FAV MEMORY OR RECOMMENDED ACTIVITY

MY MESSAGE

MAY WE SHARE YOUR MESSAGE? ☐ YES ☐ NO

Messages

GUEST NAME

DATE(S) STAYED

TRAVELING FROM

OUR FAV MEMORY OR RECOMMENDED ACTIVITY

MY MESSAGE

MAY WE SHARE YOUR MESSAGE? ☐ YES ☐ NO

Messages

GUEST NAME

DATE(S) STAYED

TRAVELING FROM

OUR FAV MEMORY OR RECOMMENDED ACTIVITY

MY MESSAGE

MAY WE SHARE YOUR MESSAGE? ☐ YES ☐ NO

Messages

GUEST NAME ______________________ DATE(S) STAYED ______________________

TRAVELING FROM ______________________

OUR FAV MEMORY OR RECOMMENDED ACTIVITY

MY MESSAGE

MAY WE SHARE YOUR MESSAGE? ☐ YES ☐ NO

Messages

GUEST NAME

DATE(S) STAYED

TRAVELING FROM

OUR FAV MEMORY OR RECOMMENDED ACTIVITY

MY MESSAGE

MAY WE SHARE YOUR MESSAGE? ☐ YES ☐ NO

Messages

GUEST NAME ______________ DATE(S) STAYED ______________

TRAVELING FROM ______________

OUR FAV MEMORY OR RECOMMENDED ACTIVITY

MY MESSAGE

MAY WE SHARE YOUR MESSAGE? ☐ YES ☐ NO

Messages

GUEST NAME ____________ DATE(S) STAYED ____________

TRAVELING FROM ____________

OUR FAV MEMORY OR RECOMMENDED ACTIVITY

MY MESSAGE

MAY WE SHARE YOUR MESSAGE? ☐ YES ☐ NO

Messages

GUEST NAME ____________ DATE(S) STAYED ____________

TRAVELING FROM ____________

OUR FAV MEMORY OR RECOMMENDED ACTIVITY

MY MESSAGE

MAY WE SHARE YOUR MESSAGE? ☐ YES ☐ NO

Messages

GUEST NAME ______________________ DATE(S) STAYED ______________________

TRAVELING FROM ______________________

OUR FAV MEMORY OR RECOMMENDED ACTIVITY

MY MESSAGE

MAY WE SHARE YOUR MESSAGE? ☐ YES ☐ NO

Messages

GUEST NAME

DATE(S) STAYED

TRAVELING FROM

OUR FAV MEMORY OR RECOMMENDED ACTIVITY

MY MESSAGE

MAY WE SHARE YOUR MESSAGE? ☐ YES ☐ NO

Messages

GUEST NAME

DATE(S) STAYED

TRAVELING FROM

OUR FAV MEMORY OR RECOMMENDED ACTIVITY

MY MESSAGE

MAY WE SHARE YOUR MESSAGE? ☐ YES ☐ NO

Messages

GUEST NAME DATE(S) STAYED

TRAVELING FROM

OUR FAV MEMORY OR RECOMMENDED ACTIVITY

MY MESSAGE

MAY WE SHARE YOUR MESSAGE? YES NO

Messages

GUEST NAME DATE(S) STAYED

TRAVELING FROM

OUR FAV MEMORY OR RECOMMENDED ACTIVITY

MY MESSAGE

MAY WE SHARE YOUR MESSAGE? ☐ YES ☐ NO

Messages

GUEST NAME ____________________ DATE(S) STAYED ____________________

TRAVELING FROM ____________________

OUR FAV MEMORY OR RECOMMENDED ACTIVITY

MY MESSAGE

MAY WE SHARE YOUR MESSAGE? ☐ YES ☐ NO

Messages

GUEST NAME

DATE(S) STAYED

TRAVELING FROM

OUR FAV MEMORY OR RECOMMENDED ACTIVITY

MY MESSAGE

MAY WE SHARE YOUR MESSAGE? ☐ YES ☐ NO

Messages

GUEST NAME DATE(S) STAYED

TRAVELING FROM

OUR FAV MEMORY OR RECOMMENDED ACTIVITY

MY MESSAGE

MAY WE SHARE YOUR MESSAGE? ☐ YES ☐ NO

Messages

GUEST NAME

DATE(S) STAYED

TRAVELING FROM

OUR FAV MEMORY OR RECOMMENDED ACTIVITY

MY MESSAGE

MAY WE SHARE YOUR MESSAGE? ☐ YES ☐ NO

Messages

GUEST NAME DATE(S) STAYED

TRAVELING FROM

OUR FAV MEMORY OR RECOMMENDED ACTIVITY

MY MESSAGE

MAY WE SHARE YOUR MESSAGE? ☐ YES ☐ NO

Messages

GUEST NAME ______ DATE(S) STAYED ______

TRAVELING FROM ______

OUR FAV MEMORY OR RECOMMENDED ACTIVITY

MY MESSAGE

MAY WE SHARE YOUR MESSAGE? ☐ YES ☐ NO

Messages

GUEST NAME ____________ DATE(S) STAYED ____________

TRAVELING FROM ____________

OUR FAV MEMORY OR RECOMMENDED ACTIVITY

MY MESSAGE

MAY WE SHARE YOUR MESSAGE? ☐ YES ☐ NO

Messages

GUEST NAME DATE(S) STAYED

TRAVELING FROM

OUR FAV MEMORY OR RECOMMENDED ACTIVITY

MY MESSAGE

MAY WE SHARE YOUR MESSAGE? ☐ YES ☐ NO

Messages

GUEST NAME DATE(S) STAYED

TRAVELING FROM

OUR FAV MEMORY OR RECOMMENDED ACTIVITY

MY MESSAGE

MAY WE SHARE YOUR MESSAGE? ☐ YES ☐ NO

Messages

GUEST NAME

DATE(S) STAYED

TRAVELING FROM

OUR FAV MEMORY OR RECOMMENDED ACTIVITY

MY MESSAGE

MAY WE SHARE YOUR MESSAGE? ☐ YES ☐ NO

Messages

GUEST NAME ______________________ DATE(S) STAYED ______________________

TRAVELING FROM ______________________

OUR FAV MEMORY OR RECOMMENDED ACTIVITY

MY MESSAGE

MAY WE SHARE YOUR MESSAGE? ☐ YES ☐ NO

Messages

GUEST NAME

DATE(S) STAYED

TRAVELING FROM

OUR FAV MEMORY OR RECOMMENDED ACTIVITY

MY MESSAGE

MAY WE SHARE YOUR MESSAGE? ☐ YES ☐ NO

Messages

GUEST NAME

DATE(S) STAYED

TRAVELING FROM

OUR FAV MEMORY OR RECOMMENDED ACTIVITY

MY MESSAGE

MAY WE SHARE YOUR MESSAGE? ☐ YES ☐ NO

Messages

GUEST NAME ____________________ DATE(S) STAYED ____________________

TRAVELING FROM ____________________

OUR FAV MEMORY OR RECOMMENDED ACTIVITY

MY MESSAGE

MAY WE SHARE YOUR MESSAGE? ☐ YES ☐ NO

Messages

GUEST NAME

DATE(S) STAYED

TRAVELING FROM

OUR FAV MEMORY OR RECOMMENDED ACTIVITY

MY MESSAGE

MAY WE SHARE YOUR MESSAGE? ☐ YES ☐ NO

Messages

GUEST NAME DATE(S) STAYED

TRAVELING FROM

OUR FAV MEMORY OR RECOMMENDED ACTIVITY

MY MESSAGE

MAY WE SHARE YOUR MESSAGE? ☐ YES ☐ NO

Messages

GUEST NAME ____________ DATE(S) STAYED ____________

TRAVELING FROM ____________

OUR FAV MEMORY OR RECOMMENDED ACTIVITY

MY MESSAGE

MAY WE SHARE YOUR MESSAGE? ☐ YES ☐ NO

Messages

GUEST NAME ______________ DATE(S) STAYED ______________

TRAVELING FROM ______________

OUR FAV MEMORY OR RECOMMENDED ACTIVITY

MY MESSAGE

MAY WE SHARE YOUR MESSAGE? ☐ YES ☐ NO

Messages

GUEST NAME

DATE(S) STAYED

TRAVELING FROM

OUR FAV MEMORY OR RECOMMENDED ACTIVITY

MY MESSAGE

MAY WE SHARE YOUR MESSAGE? ☐ YES ☐ NO

Messages

GUEST NAME

DATE(S) STAYED

TRAVELING FROM

OUR FAV MEMORY OR RECOMMENDED ACTIVITY

MY MESSAGE

MAY WE SHARE YOUR MESSAGE? ☐ YES ☐ NO

Messages

GUEST NAME ____________________ DATE(S) STAYED ____________________

TRAVELING FROM ____________________

OUR FAV MEMORY OR RECOMMENDED ACTIVITY

MY MESSAGE

MAY WE SHARE YOUR MESSAGE? ☐ YES ☐ NO

Messages

GUEST NAME ______________________ DATE(S) STAYED ______________________

TRAVELING FROM ______________________

OUR FAV MEMORY OR RECOMMENDED ACTIVITY

MY MESSAGE

MAY WE SHARE YOUR MESSAGE? ☐ YES ☐ NO

Messages

GUEST NAME DATE(S) STAYED

TRAVELING FROM

OUR FAV MEMORY OR RECOMMENDED ACTIVITY

MY MESSAGE

MAY WE SHARE YOUR MESSAGE? ☐ YES ☐ NO

Messages

GUEST NAME ____________ DATE(S) STAYED ____________

TRAVELING FROM ____________

OUR FAV MEMORY OR RECOMMENDED ACTIVITY

MY MESSAGE

MAY WE SHARE YOUR MESSAGE? ☐ YES ☐ NO

Messages

GUEST NAME

DATE(S) STAYED

TRAVELING FROM

OUR FAV MEMORY OR RECOMMENDED ACTIVITY

MY MESSAGE

MAY WE SHARE YOUR MESSAGE? ☐ YES ☐ NO

Messages

GUEST NAME

DATE(S) STAYED

TRAVELING FROM

OUR FAV MEMORY OR RECOMMENDED ACTIVITY

MY MESSAGE

MAY WE SHARE YOUR MESSAGE? ☐ YES ☐ NO

Messages

GUEST NAME

DATE(S) STAYED

TRAVELING FROM

OUR FAV MEMORY OR RECOMMENDED ACTIVITY

MY MESSAGE

MAY WE SHARE YOUR MESSAGE? ☐ YES ☐ NO

Messages

GUEST NAME ______ DATE(S) STAYED ______

TRAVELING FROM ______

OUR FAV MEMORY OR RECOMMENDED ACTIVITY

MY MESSAGE

MAY WE SHARE YOUR MESSAGE? ☐ YES ☐ NO

Messages

GUEST NAME ______________________ DATE(S) STAYED ______________________

TRAVELING FROM ______________________

OUR FAV MEMORY OR RECOMMENDED ACTIVITY

MY MESSAGE

MAY WE SHARE YOUR MESSAGE? ☐ YES ☐ NO

Messages

GUEST NAME

DATE(S) STAYED

TRAVELING FROM

OUR FAV MEMORY OR RECOMMENDED ACTIVITY

MY MESSAGE

MAY WE SHARE YOUR MESSAGE? ☐ YES ☐ NO

Messages

GUEST NAME

DATE(S) STAYED

TRAVELING FROM

OUR FAV MEMORY OR RECOMMENDED ACTIVITY

MY MESSAGE

MAY WE SHARE YOUR MESSAGE? ☐ YES ☐ NO

Messages

GUEST NAME

DATE(S) STAYED

TRAVELING FROM

OUR FAV MEMORY OR RECOMMENDED ACTIVITY

MY MESSAGE

MAY WE SHARE YOUR MESSAGE? ☐ YES ☐ NO

Messages

GUEST NAME ______________ DATE(S) STAYED ______________

TRAVELING FROM ______________

OUR FAV MEMORY OR RECOMMENDED ACTIVITY

MY MESSAGE

MAY WE SHARE YOUR MESSAGE? ☐ YES ☐ NO

Messages

GUEST NAME

DATE(S) STAYED

TRAVELING FROM

OUR FAV MEMORY OR RECOMMENDED ACTIVITY

MY MESSAGE

MAY WE SHARE YOUR MESSAGE? YES NO

Messages

GUEST NAME ______________ DATE(S) STAYED ______________

TRAVELING FROM ______________

OUR FAV MEMORY OR RECOMMENDED ACTIVITY

MY MESSAGE

MAY WE SHARE YOUR MESSAGE? ☐ YES ☐ NO

Messages

GUEST NAME

DATE(S) STAYED

TRAVELING FROM

OUR FAV MEMORY OR RECOMMENDED ACTIVITY

MY MESSAGE

MAY WE SHARE YOUR MESSAGE? ☐ YES ☐ NO

Messages

GUEST NAME

DATE(S) STAYED

TRAVELING FROM

OUR FAV MEMORY OR RECOMMENDED ACTIVITY

MY MESSAGE

MAY WE SHARE YOUR MESSAGE? ☐ YES ☐ NO

Messages

GUEST NAME

DATE(S) STAYED

TRAVELING FROM

OUR FAV MEMORY OR RECOMMENDED ACTIVITY

MY MESSAGE

MAY WE SHARE YOUR MESSAGE? ☐ YES ☐ NO

Messages

GUEST NAME

DATE(S) STAYED

TRAVELING FROM

OUR FAV MEMORY OR RECOMMENDED ACTIVITY

MY MESSAGE

MAY WE SHARE YOUR MESSAGE? ☐ YES ☐ NO

Messages

GUEST NAME

DATE(S) STAYED

TRAVELING FROM

OUR FAV MEMORY OR RECOMMENDED ACTIVITY

MY MESSAGE

MAY WE SHARE YOUR MESSAGE? YES NO

Messages

GUEST NAME

DATE(S) STAYED

TRAVELING FROM

OUR FAV MEMORY OR RECOMMENDED ACTIVITY

MY MESSAGE

MAY WE SHARE YOUR MESSAGE? ☐ YES ☐ NO

Messages

GUEST NAME

DATE(S) STAYED

TRAVELING FROM

OUR FAV MEMORY OR RECOMMENDED ACTIVITY

MY MESSAGE

MAY WE SHARE YOUR MESSAGE? ☐ YES ☐ NO

Messages

GUEST NAME ______________________ DATE(S) STAYED ______________________

TRAVELING FROM ______________________

OUR FAV MEMORY OR RECOMMENDED ACTIVITY

MY MESSAGE

MAY WE SHARE YOUR MESSAGE? ☐ YES ☐ NO

Messages

GUEST NAME

DATE(S) STAYED

TRAVELING FROM

OUR FAV MEMORY OR RECOMMENDED ACTIVITY

MY MESSAGE

MAY WE SHARE YOUR MESSAGE? ☐ YES ☐ NO

Messages

GUEST NAME

DATE(S) STAYED

TRAVELING FROM

OUR FAV MEMORY OR RECOMMENDED ACTIVITY

MY MESSAGE

MAY WE SHARE YOUR MESSAGE? ☐ YES ☐ NO

Messages

GUEST NAME

DATE(S) STAYED

TRAVELING FROM

OUR FAV MEMORY OR RECOMMENDED ACTIVITY

MY MESSAGE

MAY WE SHARE YOUR MESSAGE? ☐ YES ☐ NO

Messages

GUEST NAME ______________________ DATE(S) STAYED ______________________

TRAVELING FROM ______________________

OUR FAV MEMORY OR RECOMMENDED ACTIVITY

MY MESSAGE

MAY WE SHARE YOUR MESSAGE? ☐ YES ☐ NO

Messages

GUEST NAME

DATE(S) STAYED

TRAVELING FROM

OUR FAV MEMORY OR RECOMMENDED ACTIVITY

MY MESSAGE

MAY WE SHARE YOUR MESSAGE? ☐ YES ☐ NO

Messages

GUEST NAME ____________________ DATE(S) STAYED ____________________

TRAVELING FROM ____________________

OUR FAV MEMORY OR RECOMMENDED ACTIVITY

MY MESSAGE

MAY WE SHARE YOUR MESSAGE? ☐ YES ☐ NO

Messages

GUEST NAME ______________________ DATE(S) STAYED ______________________

TRAVELING FROM ______________________

OUR FAV MEMORY OR RECOMMENDED ACTIVITY

MY MESSAGE

MAY WE SHARE YOUR MESSAGE? ☐ YES ☐ NO

Messages

GUEST NAME

DATE(S) STAYED

TRAVELING FROM

OUR FAV MEMORY OR RECOMMENDED ACTIVITY

MY MESSAGE

MAY WE SHARE YOUR MESSAGE? ☐ YES ☐ NO

Messages

GUEST NAME DATE(S) STAYED

TRAVELING FROM

OUR FAV MEMORY OR RECOMMENDED ACTIVITY

MY MESSAGE

MAY WE SHARE YOUR MESSAGE? ☐ YES ☐ NO

Messages

GUEST NAME ______________ DATE(S) STAYED ______________

TRAVELING FROM ______________

OUR FAV MEMORY OR RECOMMENDED ACTIVITY

MY MESSAGE

MAY WE SHARE YOUR MESSAGE? ☐ YES ☐ NO

Messages

GUEST NAME ______________________ DATE(S) STAYED ______________________

TRAVELING FROM ______________________

OUR FAV MEMORY OR RECOMMENDED ACTIVITY

MY MESSAGE

MAY WE SHARE YOUR MESSAGE? ☐ YES ☐ NO

Messages

GUEST NAME

DATE(S) STAYED

TRAVELING FROM

OUR FAV MEMORY OR RECOMMENDED ACTIVITY

MY MESSAGE

MAY WE SHARE YOUR MESSAGE? ☐ YES ☐ NO

Messages

GUEST NAME

DATE(S) STAYED

TRAVELING FROM

OUR FAV MEMORY OR RECOMMENDED ACTIVITY

MY MESSAGE

MAY WE SHARE YOUR MESSAGE? ☐ YES ☐ NO

Messages

GUEST NAME ______ DATE(S) STAYED ______

TRAVELING FROM ______

OUR FAV MEMORY OR RECOMMENDED ACTIVITY

MY MESSAGE

MAY WE SHARE YOUR MESSAGE? ☐ YES ☐ NO

Messages

GUEST NAME

DATE(S) STAYED

TRAVELING FROM

OUR FAV MEMORY OR RECOMMENDED ACTIVITY

MY MESSAGE

MAY WE SHARE YOUR MESSAGE? ☐ YES ☐ NO

Messages

GUEST NAME ________________ DATE(S) STAYED ________________

TRAVELING FROM ________________

OUR FAV MEMORY OR RECOMMENDED ACTIVITY

MY MESSAGE

MAY WE SHARE YOUR MESSAGE? ☐ YES ☐ NO

Messages

GUEST NAME

DATE(S) STAYED

TRAVELING FROM

OUR FAV MEMORY OR RECOMMENDED ACTIVITY

MY MESSAGE

MAY WE SHARE YOUR MESSAGE? ☐ YES ☐ NO

Messages

GUEST NAME

DATE(S) STAYED

TRAVELING FROM

OUR FAV MEMORY OR RECOMMENDED ACTIVITY

MY MESSAGE

MAY WE SHARE YOUR MESSAGE? ☐ YES ☐ NO

Messages

GUEST NAME

DATE(S) STAYED

TRAVELING FROM

OUR FAV MEMORY OR RECOMMENDED ACTIVITY

MY MESSAGE

MAY WE SHARE YOUR MESSAGE? ☐ YES ☐ NO

Messages

GUEST NAME DATE(S) STAYED

TRAVELING FROM

OUR FAV MEMORY OR RECOMMENDED ACTIVITY

MY MESSAGE

MAY WE SHARE YOUR MESSAGE? YES NO

Messages

GUEST NAME

DATE(S) STAYED

TRAVELING FROM

OUR FAV MEMORY OR RECOMMENDED ACTIVITY

MY MESSAGE

MAY WE SHARE YOUR MESSAGE? YES NO

Messages

GUEST NAME ______ DATE(S) STAYED ______

TRAVELING FROM ______

OUR FAV MEMORY OR RECOMMENDED ACTIVITY

MY MESSAGE

MAY WE SHARE YOUR MESSAGE? ☐ YES ☐ NO

Messages

GUEST NAME ______ DATE(S) STAYED ______

TRAVELING FROM ______

OUR FAV MEMORY OR RECOMMENDED ACTIVITY

MY MESSAGE

MAY WE SHARE YOUR MESSAGE? ☐ YES ☐ NO

Messages

GUEST NAME

DATE(S) STAYED

TRAVELING FROM

OUR FAV MEMORY OR RECOMMENDED ACTIVITY

MY MESSAGE

MAY WE SHARE YOUR MESSAGE? ☐ YES ☐ NO

Messages

GUEST NAME ______________________ DATE(S) STAYED ______________________

TRAVELING FROM ______________________

OUR FAV MEMORY OR RECOMMENDED ACTIVITY

MY MESSAGE

MAY WE SHARE YOUR MESSAGE? ☐ YES ☐ NO

Messages

GUEST NAME ______________________ DATE(S) STAYED ______________________

TRAVELING FROM ______________________

OUR FAV MEMORY OR RECOMMENDED ACTIVITY

MY MESSAGE

MAY WE SHARE YOUR MESSAGE? ☐ YES ☐ NO

Messages

GUEST NAME ______________________ DATE(S) STAYED ______________________

TRAVELING FROM ______________________

OUR FAV MEMORY OR RECOMMENDED ACTIVITY

MY MESSAGE

MAY WE SHARE YOUR MESSAGE? ☐ YES ☐ NO

Messages

GUEST NAME

DATE(S) STAYED

TRAVELING FROM

OUR FAV MEMORY OR RECOMMENDED ACTIVITY

MY MESSAGE

MAY WE SHARE YOUR MESSAGE? ☐ YES ☐ NO

Messages

GUEST NAME

DATE(S) STAYED

TRAVELING FROM

OUR FAV MEMORY OR RECOMMENDED ACTIVITY

MY MESSAGE

MAY WE SHARE YOUR MESSAGE? ☐ YES ☐ NO

Messages

GUEST NAME ______ DATE(S) STAYED ______

TRAVELING FROM ______

OUR FAV MEMORY OR RECOMMENDED ACTIVITY

MY MESSAGE

MAY WE SHARE YOUR MESSAGE? ☐ YES ☐ NO

Messages

GUEST NAME

DATE(S) STAYED

TRAVELING FROM

OUR FAV MEMORY OR RECOMMENDED ACTIVITY

MY MESSAGE

MAY WE SHARE YOUR MESSAGE? ☐ YES ☐ NO

Messages

GUEST NAME ______ DATE(S) STAYED ______

TRAVELING FROM ______

OUR FAV MEMORY OR RECOMMENDED ACTIVITY

MY MESSAGE

MAY WE SHARE YOUR MESSAGE? ☐ YES ☐ NO

Messages

GUEST NAME ______________________ DATE(S) STAYED ______________________

TRAVELING FROM ______________________

OUR FAV MEMORY OR RECOMMENDED ACTIVITY

MY MESSAGE

MAY WE SHARE YOUR MESSAGE? ☐ YES ☐ NO

Messages

GUEST NAME

DATE(S) STAYED

TRAVELING FROM

OUR FAV MEMORY OR RECOMMENDED ACTIVITY

MY MESSAGE

MAY WE SHARE YOUR MESSAGE? ☐ YES ☐ NO

Messages

GUEST NAME

DATE(S) STAYED

TRAVELING FROM

OUR FAV MEMORY OR RECOMMENDED ACTIVITY

MY MESSAGE

MAY WE SHARE YOUR MESSAGE? ☐ YES ☐ NO

Messages

GUEST NAME ______________________ DATE(S) STAYED ______________________

TRAVELING FROM ______________________

OUR FAV MEMORY OR RECOMMENDED ACTIVITY

MY MESSAGE

MAY WE SHARE YOUR MESSAGE? ☐ YES ☐ NO

Messages

GUEST NAME

DATE(S) STAYED

TRAVELING FROM

OUR FAV MEMORY OR RECOMMENDED ACTIVITY

MY MESSAGE

MAY WE SHARE YOUR MESSAGE? ☐ YES ☐ NO

Messages

GUEST NAME

DATE(S) STAYED

TRAVELING FROM

OUR FAV MEMORY OR RECOMMENDED ACTIVITY

MY MESSAGE

MAY WE SHARE YOUR MESSAGE? ☐ YES ☐ NO

Messages

GUEST NAME

DATE(S) STAYED

TRAVELING FROM

OUR FAV MEMORY OR RECOMMENDED ACTIVITY

MY MESSAGE

MAY WE SHARE YOUR MESSAGE? ☐ YES ☐ NO

Messages

GUEST NAME

DATE(S) STAYED

TRAVELING FROM

OUR FAV MEMORY OR RECOMMENDED ACTIVITY

MY MESSAGE

MAY WE SHARE YOUR MESSAGE? ☐ YES ☐ NO

Messages

GUEST NAME ______________________ DATE(S) STAYED ______________________

TRAVELING FROM ______________________

OUR FAV MEMORY OR RECOMMENDED ACTIVITY

MY MESSAGE

MAY WE SHARE YOUR MESSAGE? ☐ YES ☐ NO

Messages

GUEST NAME

DATE(S) STAYED

TRAVELING FROM

OUR FAV MEMORY OR RECOMMENDED ACTIVITY

MY MESSAGE

MAY WE SHARE YOUR MESSAGE? ☐ YES ☐ NO

Messages

GUEST NAME ______________________ DATE(S) STAYED ______________________

TRAVELING FROM ______________________

OUR FAV MEMORY OR RECOMMENDED ACTIVITY

MY MESSAGE

MAY WE SHARE YOUR MESSAGE? ☐ YES ☐ NO

Messages

GUEST NAME

DATE(S) STAYED

TRAVELING FROM

OUR FAV MEMORY OR RECOMMENDED ACTIVITY

MY MESSAGE

MAY WE SHARE YOUR MESSAGE? ☐ YES ☐ NO